Will   Irma   Taranee   Cornelia   Hay Lin

CRUSHES

Will · Irma · Taranee · Cornelia · Hay Lin

CRUSHES

HarperCollins *Children's Books*

First published in the USA by Volo/Hyperion Books for Children.

First published in Great Britain in 2006 by HarperCollins Children's Books.
HarperCollins Children's Books is a division of HarperCollins Publishers Ltd.

The HarperCollins Children's Books website is at
www.harpercollinschildrensbooks.co.uk

ISBN: 0-00-723268-3
ISBN-13: 978-000-723268-0

1 2 3 4 5 6 7 8 9 10

The HarperCollins Children's Books website is at
www.harpercollinschildrensbooks.co.uk

Printed and bound in Italy

Visit www.clubwitch.co.uk

CONTENTS

CHAPTER ONE
LOVE IS . . .

⑥ *Tuesday morning*
Outside school

Irma: Hi, girls! Have you heard the latest news?

Cornelia: No, what's going on?

Irma: You know Tom, right?

Hay Lin: Sure. He's supercute!

Irma: He and Karen broke up.

Will: What? How do you know?

Irma: I've got eyes, and I use them! Besides, "Radio Sheffield" Sarah confirmed it. Just say hi to her and she starts gabbing about everyone and everything.

Will: I bet Karen's pretty bummed. They seemed like a cute couple.

Irma: Who cares? The important thing is that Tom's free now, and ready to start going out with other girls!

Taranee: I've heard he's kind of stuck-up.

Irma: Says who? It would be great to have him as boyfriend.

1

Hay Lin: I think Taranee has a point. I wouldn't go out with a guy just because he was the cutest or most popular or whatever. What about his personality? What about his heart? I'm an incurable romantic.

Irma: No doubt about it.

Hay Lin: Irma, you're totally out of it. Love is . . . important.

Irma: Love? I think we'd better choose our words carefully here. Aren't we still too young? We're talking about crushes. Big, small, intense – they're still *just crushes*!

Cornelia (sighing): Some get crushes, others get *crushed*.

Irma: In your case, Corny, I'd say *completely squashed*.

Taranee, Will, and Hay Lin throw Irma dirty looks. . . .

Irma: *Ahem*, what I meant was . . . Sorry, Cornelia, I guess you were pretty upset about Caleb!

Will: Irma!

Irma: What? I said I was sorry! Though, if you ask me, you're all taking this love thing way too seriously.

Cornelia: Irma, when you fall in love . . .

Irma: . . . You become a total zombie!

Cornelia: What I wanted to say was, when you're in love, the whole world seems so much more beautiful! You wake up in the morning and, strangely, you feel great!

Will: True! You feel different. How can I describe it? Lighter and . . .

Taranee: . . . You feel like laughing . . . or crying. . . .

Irma: Listen up, members of the LOVE CLUB! Maybe you're right, but you always seem to wind up crying on poor Irma's shoulder because your boyfriends are driving you up the wall!

Taranee: That's all part of it, Irma. Love is so cool because it's the spice of life. Having a boyfriend means good times . . . and problems, too. Because he makes you jealous, because he makes you mad, because he forgets to phone you . . .

Irma: Okay, I get the picture! But, please, girls: chill out. I'm going to be extra careful when it comes to picking out a boyfriend. After all, I want to avoid tear-filled afternoons at all costs.

Cornelia: Okay, Irma. Since you are such a love expert, let's have a rundown of your ideal boy's best qualities.

Irma: He's good-looking, fun to be with, intelligent, sweet, and caring. . . .

Will: Don't be too picky, Irma . . . otherwise you may not ever find Mr. Right. You may fall for a boy without even knowing why!

He's the exact opposite of everything you've been dreaming of, and yet as soon as he comes near you your heart starts beating like crazy, and you turn a hundred shades of red, and . . .

Irma: At that point, a good joke always helps!

Will: Come on, I bet there are plenty of crush situations where even you would lose your sense of humour.

Irma: Girls, you are making this into too big a deal. I'm fine!

Cornelia: Is there something you're not telling us?

Irma: Yes! It's just that I'm the Queen of Self-Control!

THE ORACLE SAYS...

Having a crush on somebody can be wonderful, but it has its ups and downs. Sometimes you feel as if you're walking on air, and the next moment you can be dragging your feet through the mud. When you like someone, everything that person does feels special.

SO, HOW CAN A GIRL IN LOVE KEEP HER FEET ON THE GROUND?

The best way is to be yourself. Don't give up your hobbies and friends on account of a boy, because they can be lifelines when you're caught up in the stormy seas of love.

HE'S WORTHY OF A CRUSH IF . . .

❧ He doesn't stand you up and doesn't use lame excuses when he has to cancel a date.

❧ He knows how to listen to you, and makes you laugh.

❧ He's happy to hear from you whenever you call, even if he's watching his favourite team in action on TV.

❧ He doesn't ignore you when he's with his friends.

FIVE WAYS TO GET ALONG WITH YOUR BOYFRIEND

 **WILL:** When you are together, always try to be yourself.

IRMA: Ask friends for advice.

 **TARANEE:** Trust him . . . but never 100 percent!

CORNELIA: Avoid overanalyzing the situation, and just have fun!

 **HAY LIN:** Try to amaze him every time you are together!

CHAPTER TWO
CUPID STRIKES AGAIN

⑥ *Monday morning*
At Sheffield Institute

Irma, Taranee, and Hay Lin meet between classes.

Irma: **I've got a problem!**

Hay Lin: What? Is everything okay?

Irma: **I think I'm in love!**

Hay Lin: Whaaat? The other day you were going on and on about how we're too *young* for love, and now . . .

Irma: **Well, I take it all back!**

Taranee: What happened?

Irma: **Yesterday I was hanging out with Lisa. Remember her? Her dad works at the station with my dad.**

Hay Lin: The one who plays basketball?

Irma: **Yes! So, we went to see a basketball game with some of her friends. And . . . the cutest boy I've ever seen was there!**

8

Taranee: Wow! Ladies and gentlemen, introducing Irma, who's officially been bitten by the love bug! Wait till the others hear this. . . .

Irma: Be serious! You've got to help me! I need advice, and fast, from anyone willing to lend a hand, even Cornelia. I've got to meet this guy, if it's the last thing I do!

Hay Lin: What do you mean? Didn't Lisa introduce you to him?

Irma: I wish! That would have been too easy! She didn't know who he was.

Taranee: So what's the big deal? Just ask one of Lisa's friends to introduce you.

Just then, Will and Cornelia walk up.

Will: . . . Introduce you to whom?

Cornelia: Have we missed something?

Taranee: Huge news, my friends. Irma's fallen head over heels in love with a basketball player!

Cornelia: So, Miss I'll-Never-Fall-In-Love has fallen? I don't believe it!

Irma: All I said was that he's cute. . . .

Hay Lin: Don't lie! You said he was – and I quote – "the cutest boy I've ever seen. . . ."

Irma: Hay Lin, what are you doing, taking notes?

Will: Let's stop fighting and get back to the topic of conversation. So, the deal is – Irma, you like a guy and you want your friend Lisa to introduce you, right?

Irma: **Right. At least, that's what Taranee suggested.**

Will: I disagree. Don't get other people involved unless absolutely necessary.

Irma: **So what do I do? All I know is that he plays basketball.**

Will: Well, that's something! Go watch more games – sooner or later he's bound to notice you.

Cornelia: **I don't know . . . I think it's good to let destiny run its course, but sometimes it needs a nudge. I'd try to get him to notice me, or think up some excuse to get near him.**

Irma: Yeah, like, "Sorry, but do you know what time it is?"

Cornelia: **Sure, start out with something simple. All you need to do is break the ice. Then you can hit him with something like, "You're a really great player! Where did you learn your moves?"**

Irma: Well . . . actually, he's the worst guy on the team. *But* he makes all the other guys laugh! And he's got this puppy-dog smile!

Just then the bell rings, and the girls head back to class. The next day, the friends meet between classes. . . .

Irma: Hey, so do you want to hear the latest?

Will, Cornelia, Hay Lin, and Taranee: Su-u-ure!

Irma: I did it! I met him!

Will: Really? That's amazing! Tell us *everything*.

Irma: I did just what Cornelia said – I know, shocking. I went straight up to him with a silly excuse to start talking.

Hay Lin: When?

Irma: On the way home from school yesterday. I stopped by the gym where his team practises, and when I saw him walk out the door I told him what a nice shirt he was wearing, and asked where he'd bought it.

Hay Lin: You're a genius, Irma!

Irma: Thank you very much! He was so nice, and told me to call him Steve, like all his friends do. Isn't that a cool name?

Cornelia: You are so in love. . . .

Irma: I told him about how I had seen him in action . . . and then we started talking about a bunch of other stuff, especially music. We have the same tastes. And then, before saying good-bye – he invited me to come see him play on Sunday.

Taranee and Hay Lin: Nice going! Sounds like things are going well.

Irma: But what about my next move? What do I do?

Taranee: Try to talk to him as much as possible. That way you'll find out if you really like him!

Irma: I already know I like him, *a lot!*

Cornelia: Just remember, you've only spoken to this guy once. But, if you're sure about your feelings, try to let him know . . . without overdoing it.

Irma: How?

Cornelia (smiling): Try an extra smile or two, and sweeten up your tone when you talk to him. You've got to show him who you are. That's a must . . . and something you deserve!

The girls meet Sunday at Irma's house.

Cornelia, Taranee, and Will: So, Irma, how'd it go?

Hay Lin: Did you see him at the game? Tell us everything! That way you'll find out if you really like him!

Irma: Oh, it went all right, only . . .

Cornelia: Irma, time to plug in your brain!

Irma: Put a sock in it, Cornelia! I'm in no mood. . . . Well, after the game today we had a long talk, and I followed all of your instructions: I was myself – perhaps a little better than usual – and in the end he asked for my phone number!

Hay Lin: Fantastic, Irma! So why the long face?

Irma: Because . . . he's leaving tomorrow. He's moving!

Taranee: Well, you can always call or e-mail.

Irma: Yeah, but it's not the same thing!

Hay Lin: It's what a lot of people do. There's this friend of mine . . .

Irma: Thanks for all the help, but I still feel like the unluckiest girl in the world! Only a jinx like me . . .

Hay Lin: Poor Irma! Don't let it get you down. Look on the bright side: you've still got Martin!

Irma: Oh, no! I'd rather be a lifetime member of the Old Maids' Society than have Martin for my boyfriend!

Hay Lin, Will, Taranee, and Cornelia (all together): Ha-ha-ha!

DEAR IRMA

Advice from Irma will leave you with a smile on your face. See how she solves your problems!

Dear Irma,
How can I get a high-tech boy to notice me?
– Lost in Digital

Dear Lost in Digital,
Send him an e-mail! And add one of those fun smiley faces. Humour can come across . . . even on computers!
♥ Irma

Dear Irma,
At a costume party my crush didn't even know I was alive. How can I grab his attention?
– Wallflower

Dear Wallflower,
Trust yourself, and be *confident*. Guys love that! So next time, try a fun outfit that will really turn his head . . . and heart!
♥ Irma

Dear Irma,
I'm dying to find out all I can about a boy I like.
Any suggestions?
– Need Info

Dear Need Info,
Contact your local private eye! Just kidding. Try
asking him. . . . Sometimes you'd be surprised
how flattered guys are when girls really try to get
to know them.
♥ Irma

Dear Irma,
How does Cupid's arrow get a bull's-eye every time?
And why hasn't it hit me?
– Looking for Love

Dear Looking for Love,
Cupid has had a lot of target practise. And he
always hits you when you're least expecting it –
so stop looking, and be patient. He might have
you in his aim now!
♥ Irma

WHAT CAN YOU DO IF . . .

You don't know how to meet a boy you like?

- Make yourself more available. When in a group, avoid clinging to your friends – it may discourage *him* from coming over to talk to you.
- Find out where he hangs out . . . and just *happen* to be there, too!
- Make the first move yourself – find an excuse to talk to *him*.

You meet a cute boy, but you don't know whether you *like* him – like him or just think he's nice?

● Try to spend time talking with him. The better you get to know him, the easier it will be to figure out whether he's right for you!

● Be patient . . . you'll know soon enough. But be careful – don't fool yourself into liking someone just because you want to be in love!

17

You really like him but aren't sure how to let him know?

- Use the up-front method and simply come right out and say it. (However, keep in mind that this technique may backfire if he tells you he doesn't feel the same way.)
- Try the subtle approach, sending sweet glances his way or dropping a few hints. If he doesn't catch on, he's probably not the boy for you, and you've avoided any embarrassing situations.
- Play hard-to-get and wait for him to make the first move. The only problem with this method is that sometimes waiting can get boring. So while you wait, remember: there are other fish in the sea.

18

CHAPTER THREE
MAYDAY... MAYDAY... FIRST DATE ALERT!

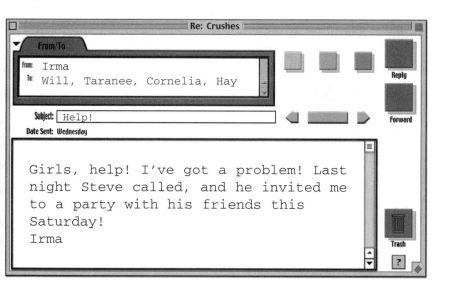

Re: Crushes

From/To

From: Irma
To: Will, Taranee, Cornelia, Hay

Reply

Subject: Help!

Date Sent: Wednesday

Forward

Girls, help! I've got a problem! Last night Steve called, and he invited me to a party with his friends this Saturday!
Irma

Trash

?

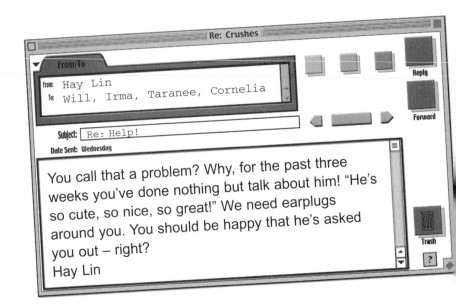

Re: Crushes

From/To

From: Hay Lin
To: Will, Irma, Taranee, Cornelia

Subject: Re: Help!
Date Sent: Wednesday

You call that a problem? Why, for the past three weeks you've done nothing but talk about him! "He's so cute, so nice, so great!" We need earplugs around you. You should be happy that he's asked you out – right?
Hay Lin

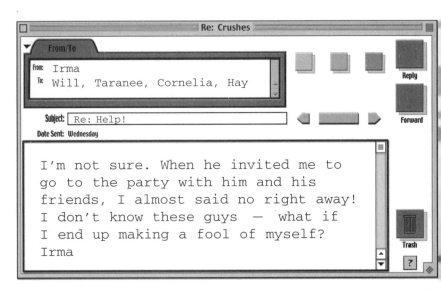

Re: Crushes

From/To

From: Irma
To: Will, Taranee, Cornelia, Hay

Subject: Re: Help!
Date Sent: Wednesday

I'm not sure. When he invited me to go to the party with him and his friends, I almost said no right away! I don't know these guys — what if I end up making a fool of myself?
Irma

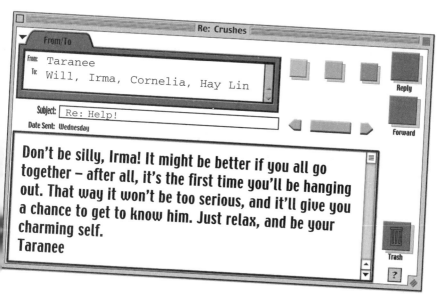

Re: Crushes

From: Taranee
To: Will, Irma, Cornelia, Hay Lin

Subject: Re: Help!
Date Sent: Wednesday

Don't be silly, Irma! It might be better if you all go together – after all, it's the first time you'll be hanging out. That way it won't be too serious, and it'll give you a chance to get to know him. Just relax, and be your charming self.
Taranee

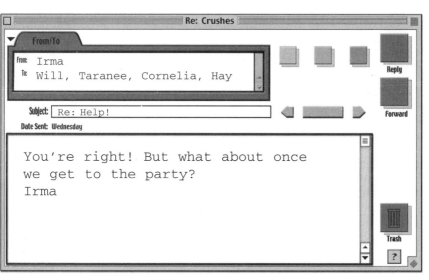

Re: Crushes

From: Irma
To: Will, Taranee, Cornelia, Hay

Subject: Re: Help!
Date Sent: Wednesday

You're right! But what about once we get to the party?
Irma

Re: Crushes

From: Hay Lin
To: Will, Irma, Taranee, Cornelia

Subject: Re: Help!
Date Sent: Wednesday

Don't worry about that – focus on the fact that he asked _you_ out!
Hay Lin

Reply

Forward

Trash
?

Re: Crushes

From: Will
To: Irma, Taranee, Cornelia, Hay Lin

Subject: Re: Help!
Date Sent: Wednesday

You like hanging out with him.
Have fun!
Will

Reply

Forward

Trash
?

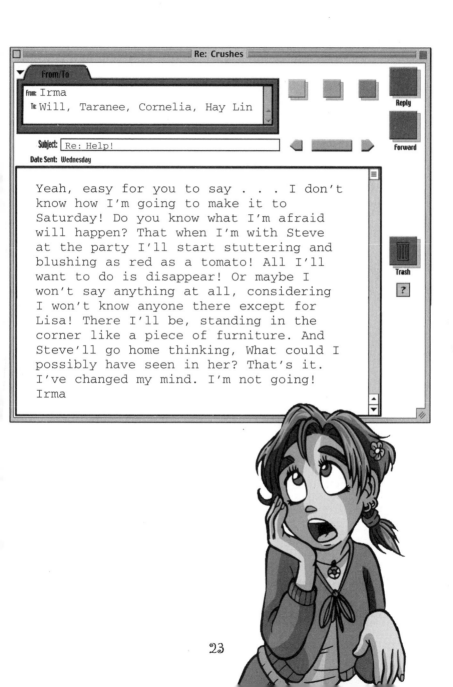

Re: Crushes

From/To

from: Irma
To: Will, Taranee, Cornelia, Hay Lin

Subject: Re: Help!
Date Sent: Wednesday

Yeah, easy for you to say . . . I don't
know how I'm going to make it to
Saturday! Do you know what I'm afraid
will happen? That when I'm with Steve
at the party I'll start stuttering and
blushing as red as a tomato! All I'll
want to do is disappear! Or maybe I
won't say anything at all, considering
I won't know anyone there except for
Lisa! There I'll be, standing in the
corner like a piece of furniture. And
Steve'll go home thinking, What could I
possibly have seen in her? That's it.
I've changed my mind. I'm not going!
Irma

Reply

Forward

Trash

?

23

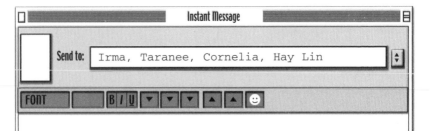
Will: Don't panic! Listen, here are a few pointers that will help you avoid **FDP**. (First Date Panic). I recommend learning these little gems by heart!

TO AVOID FDP:

Don't think . . .

- about all the things that could go wrong.
- that everything you say and do has to be smart or witty.
- that you're competing with the other girls in the group.

Think . . .

- about how glad you are to be going out with HIM.
- about how much fun you're going to have.
- about how original you are!

Buddy   Info   **SEND**

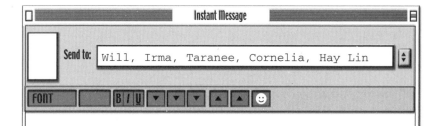

Send to: Will, Irma, Taranee, Cornelia, Hay Lin

FONT   B I U ▼ ▼ ▼ ▲ ▲ ☺

Hay Lin: I agree with Will! You need to be more self-confident, Irma. You're strong, and you're one of the cutest, nicest, most amazing girls I know. No doubt Steve has already figured this out for himself; otherwise he wouldn't have asked you out. Right?

Cornelia: Hay Lin's right, but I'd like to focus on another issue here. When it comes to first dates, fashion is superimportant. Some serious thought has to go into what you'll wear. Rule number one: nothing too flashy. Keep it comfortable, or you'll end up paying more attention to your clothes than your date. Rule number two: make the most of what you've got. A black skirt goes a long way. And what about your fuchsia top, the one with the heart on it? That's fun!

Buddy   Info   SEND

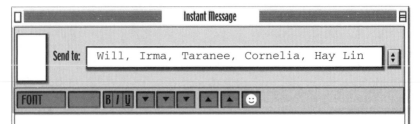

FONT   B / U

Irma: The top with the heart on it? Do you really think so? It's not too dorky?

Taranee: Don't stress, Irma! Do you remember the first time I went on a date with Nigel? It was totally nerve-racking! My heart was beating a mile a minute. But it all worked out. Later, Nigel admitted that he liked the fact that I was so shy, and he blushed every time he looked at me!

SEND

Buddy   Info

Send to: Will, Irma, Taranee, Cornelia, Hay Lin

FONT | B I U ▼ ▼ ▼ ▲ ▲ ☺

Will: And I still get jittery every time I see Matt!

Irma: I see what you guys are saying. It's going to be hard, but I'll try staying calm. Thanks for helping me through FDP - you're the best!

Instant Message

Send to: Will, Irma, Taranee, Cornelia, Hay Lin

FONT B I U ▼ ▼ ▼ ▲ ▲ ☺

Cornelia: Sounds like a good idea . . . So, until Saturday – good luck, everybody! We're going to need it, with Irma in MPM (Maximum Panic Mode)!

Irma: You must be joking! You can't abandon me!

Hay Lin: She's right! We can't. It's in situations like these that you find out who your true friends are!
P.S.: Don't forget to call me before the big date so we can go over the anti-FDP instructions!

SEND

Buddy Info

DEAR CORNELIA

Cornelia always has her head on straight. Check out her calm and classy answers to your love questions.

Dear Cornelia,
Are first dates always awkward?
– Shy Girl

Dear Shy Girl,
I'm not going to lie – they can be awkward. But it gives you something to laugh about . . . on your second date!
❀ Cornelia

Dear Cornelia,
On first dates my knees always shake, and my tongue gets tied. What should I do?
– Tied Up

Dear Tied Up,
Are you sure you're talking about first dates and not history exams? Seriously, just relax. And remember: your date is probably just as nervous as you are!
❀ Cornelia

Dear Cornelia,
I hang out with a lot of guys, but not one of them
wants to be my boyfriend. Why?
– Tomboy in Trouble

Dear Tomboy in Trouble,
Maybe you need to show those boys that you can
be a girlie-girl – they probably just need to see it
to believe it!
❀ Cornelia

Dear Cornelia,
Where's the best place to go on a first date?
– Clueless

Dear Clueless,
Anywhere is fine, as long as it's away from your
mum's (and nosy friends') eagle eyes!
❀ Cornelia

CHAPTER FOUR

WHAT IF HE DOESN'T LIKE YOU?

⊙ *Saturday*
Downtown Heatherfield

Irma: So, what do we want to do today?

Cornelia: We could always do a little window-shopping!

Irma: Surprise, surprise. You have a serious fashion obsession. If you don't watch out, you are going to turn into a fashion model one of these days. Hey, Corny. . . . Cornelia? What's wrong? It looks like you've seen a ghost. . . .

Cornelia: It's nothing, really. Let's just get out of here. . . . Oh, no! Too late!

A boy walks up to Cornelia. . . .

Tommy: Cornelia? I can't believe it's you!

Cornelia: Hi, Tommy. What are you doing here?

Tommy: I'm back home for the weekend. Life on campus is cool, but being away at boarding school can get tough sometimes.

Cornelia: I bet. Look, Tommy, I've got to get going. It was nice seeing you again. Bye!

Cornelia walks off in a hurry, dragging the others along with her.

Taranee: Corny, are you crazy? Why would you blow off a hunk like that – especially without introducing him to your friends. Who was he?

Cornelia: Just some guy I know.

Irma: Just some guy?! Okay, it's your choice: either you confess of your own free will or we torture you until you tell us everything.

Cornelia: There's *nothing* to confess. So, do you all want to head back to my place to hang out?

Will, Irma, Taranee, and Hay Lin: Sounds good!

Irma (without letting Cornelia hear her): Perfect – We've got a mystery to solve!

A little later, in Cornelia's room.

Taranee: So . . . what's the big deal with Tommy, anyway? Maybe it would be good to talk to us about it. You are obviously upset!

Cornelia: It's just that seeing him again, all of a

sudden like that, really threw me for a
loop. Tommy was my first real crush, and
he totally ditched me.

Irma: What? Ditched you? That's crazy! What
happened?

Cornelia: I met him skating a few years ago. He
was a few years older, and I thought he
was *so* great. I told him I liked him, and
he started teasing me, saying he was too
grown-up to be chasing after little kids
like me. I was so embarrassed . . . and
hurt.

Will: Poor Cornelia. It stinks to be turned down
by a guy you like, but everything always
works out and you end up feeling better.

Irma: Oh, please! If Matt dumped you, you'd
need an entire medical staff wielding
oxygen tanks to revive you!

Will: Yeah – I'd be upset, but then I'd get over it.

Taranee: A boy you like may not feel the same way
about you, but that's no reason to get
totally down. You can't lose your pride –
you are better off without him.

Irma: And it's true, time does heal all wounds.
Look at yourself – when he rejected you,
you probably wanted to disappear from the
face of the earth. But now, look – you're
here with us, joking about it. . . .

Cornelia: I guess you're right, Irma. I learned that self-esteem is really important, and that if someone rejects me, he evidently never deserved me in the first place. So . . . too bad for him!

Will: That's what I like to hear! I propose that as our motto for all the I-don't-like-you guys we ever happen to come across in the future!

Cornelia: Let's hope they're few!

THE ORACLE SAYS . . .

It's hard to accept the fact that you'll just have to wait until you meet that special someone who appreciates you for what you are. But when you do, the wait will have been well worth it!

TIPS ON SURVIVING THE DREADED WORDS "I'M NOT INTO YOU."

If you can't stop thinking of *him, him, him,* block those thoughts from your mind! Here are some good ideas to try. . . .

- Grab your diary and a pen and write your troubles away!

- If necessary, send your friends an SOS and ask for their help in distracting you.

- Remember: he said no to you – he doesn't realise the opportunity he blew!

- Steer clear of gooey romantic films for a while, or the tears may really start to flow. At times like these, action films and comedies usually work best.

- Look around: perhaps there's another boy whom you haven't noticed who's got his eye on you. . . .

CHAPTER FIVE
THE COMPETITION'S TOUGH

FROM TARANEE'S DIARY:

◎ *Tuesday*

Help! Today a girl I know told me Martina likes Nigel. Who's Martina? I need to do some research and find out this girl's story.

◎ *Wednesday*

Mission accomplished! Today at lunch I told Irma about Martina, and in just minutes I got the lowdown on the girl. She's about my height, with long hair, wears lots of makeup, and is always dressed well. In other words . . . she's perfect! Irma also told me that as soon as Martina spotted Nigel, she and one of her friends ran up to him and started chatting away. I still haven't seen this girl, but I'm already super-intimidated. What am I going to do?

⑥ *Thursday*

I spotted Martina on the way out of school! Irma's right, she's really pretty! She kept flipping her hair around, and she has this superbright smile. What if Nigel likes that? I saw them talking together today, too. I feel awful!

⑥ *Thursday night*

This afternoon I met up with my friends. I told them all about Martina, and they gave me some advice. Cornelia says I'm wrong to stay away from Nigel now that Martina is prowling around. She says I need to stand up for myself. Hay Lin says Martina's got nothing on me – she is cute, but so phony! What could Nigel possibly see in her?!

⑥ *Friday, lunchtime*

This morning I decided to go right up and say hi to Nigel as soon as I got to school . . . but Martina was already there, waiting for him in front of his locker. I'm sure she'd seen me coming and that she ran to get there before I did.

Cornelia was right: I've got to be more aggressive. Martina's about to see me spring into action!

 ### *Friday evening*

Yes! I made contact! This afternoon, on the way home from Irma's, I ran into Nigel. He was supernice to me. And so I had to ask about Martina. I said, all casually, "Is she a friend of yours?" He laughed and said she was a major phony! And then, as we were saying good-bye, he said, "Why don't you come by my class on Monday and we can walk to lunch together?" I even managed to answer him without sounding silly! Of course, I immediately called Cornelia, who gave me a pep talk. She said that if Martina is around when I'm supposed to meet Nigel on Monday, I should just ignore it and talk to Nigel. There's no way I should let her see me back down.

Monday

Today I went to see Nigel before lunch, and of course, there *she* was! I gathered my courage and went up to Nigel, with my heart pounding. Luckily, Nigel smiled at me as soon as he saw me coming. He seemed kind of busy, so I just said a quick hi and left. But the way Nigel said, "See you later!" and winked at me was so sweet! I realised then that Nigel likes me for me and that I have nothing to worry about – even from Martina!

TIPS FOR STAYING IN THE GAME WHEN YOU ARE CRUSHING:

WILL: You like your crush for who he is . . . . Chances are he feels the same about you.

IRMA: Keep it fun! Don't be too serious, or you might scare him away.

TARANEE: Your crush is only human – don't flip out if he messes up . . . once in a while!

CORNELIA: You are amazing! Your crush had better remember that.

HAY LIN: Show him how you feel with something handmade – he'll like the personal touch.

WHAT CAN YOU DO IF ...

Another girl's got eyes for your boyfriend?

● Try to find out *how* she likes him! If she has a crush on him, don't overreact. He is going out with you, so he probably doesn't even notice her – don't bring it to his attention!

● Talk to him about it, and let him know his friendship with another girl intimidates you, but that as long as you are honest with each other it should be okay.

● If she keeps chasing him, politely tell her that, while you've got nothing against the two of them being friends, she needs to remember he's *your* boyfriend.

You find out your boyfriend's got eyes for another girl?

● Keep calm. Fits of jealousy are useless and may only serve to make his attraction for the other girl grow.

● Let him know how much he means to you, and that you're not willing to play

second fiddle to anyone. Remember
that you have to lay it all on the line,
even if you're frightened of losing him.
 • If he really wants her, he can have
her. Dump him!

CHAPTER SIX
FRIENDS . . .
IN LOVE

FROM CORNELIA'S DIARY

⑤ Friday

Wow! Tomorrow we're leaving for the mountains, and I'll get to see my vacation friends again – Margaret, Michael, and the rest of the crew. I'm so excited! We don't see each other for months at a time, but as soon as we get back together it's as if no time has passed. Margaret, Michael, and I are an inseparable trio. We've been great friends ever since we were little! It's going to be fantastic to see them again!

⑤ Sunday

So we all met up in the tiny town square, as usual. Margaret was the only one missing, but everyone said she'd be here in another week.

This year Michael and I seem tighter than ever. We hang out all the time, talking our heads off . . . about school and our friends back home. Michael asked me if I had a boyfriend. He seemed happy when I said no. Odd. We wound up having a water fight, and even though I won, Michael still bought me some ice cream. He's a great guy!

Friday

I have the funny feeling that Michael's acting differently toward me. I've caught him gazing at me with a weird expression, and he's started saying things he's never said before, like how beautiful he thinks I am, and about how often he thinks of me. . . . I can't figure him out. Good thing Margaret's supposed to show up tomorrow. Things should get back to normal once the old trio's together again.

Saturday

Margaret got here this morning. Michael and I waited for her in front of her house, as we do every year. After helping her bring her bags inside, we went right out for one of our traditional tell-me-everything walks. Later, when it was just the two of us, Margaret asked if everything was okay with Michael and me. When I asked her what she was talking about, she told me it was obvious – Michael's got a crush on ME! I can't believe it! Margaret was able to see in just a couple of hours what I'd been unable to see this whole time! What's going on? Michael and I grew up together, and now . . . no, I can't believe it. I don't know what to do! Can Michael really like me?

⑥ Sunday

Unfortunately, Margaret was right. It's obvious Michael's got a thing for me! I was blind not to see it before! He's been so kind and polite to me, always paying me compliments and wanting to spend time with me. I have no clue how to handle this. If it was any other guy, I'd know just what to do – I'd let him know flat out that I don't want anything to do with him, and that would be it, plain and simple. Only with Michael, it's different. Margaret says I have to make him understand that he is and will continue to be a great friend. But it won't be as easy as it sounds. I don't want to hurt him. This is going to be a tricky situation – talk about unlucky in love!!

⑥ *Sunday evening*

Yikes! This afternoon, exactly what I didn't want to have happen, happened. Michael asked me to go for a walk with him (alone!) and then he told me he was in love with me. I didn't know what to say. I tried to be sincere, I explained that I think he's great, but that as far as I'm concerned nothing has changed between us, that we're just *friends*. You could totally tell he was hurt. I feel like such a creep.

⑥ *Monday*

Margaret came over last night, and I told her everything. It was good to get it off my chest. I have to realise that for now, Michael will probably try to keep his distance from me. All I can do is give him time and show him that I still want him as a friend, even if in the beginning it might be awkward. Sooner or later he'll come back to being my friend!

THE ORACLE SAYS...

When you develop a close relationship with a boy, doubts may often arise: is he just a friend, or is there something more? The most important thing to remember when it comes to your feelings is clarity. Send out a few initial signals to see whether he might feel the same way. If his attitude toward you seems to be changing as well, romance may be just around the corner.

CORNELIA'S TIPS

If your best guy friend gets a crush on you . . .

♣ Try to let him know you don't feel the same way *before* he actually admits his feelings. You could start talking about a crush you have – on another guy! He'll get the picture.

♣ If he does tell you he's in love with you, reply with tact and sensitivity. Remember to be clear and sincere. Leave no room for false hope!

♣ Don't go telling the whole world he's declared his love for you. Think about his feelings and what he is going through.

CHAPTER SEVEN

THE GREEN-EYED MONSTER

⑥ *Saturday*
In the park

Taranee, Cornelia, and Hay Lin: **Hi, Will!**

Will: Grrrr!

Hay Lin: **Come again!**

Will: Grrrrrrrrrrrr!

Hay Lin: **Oh, "Grrrr" must mean Matt! You've been bitten by the old jealousy bug again.**

Taranee: Last week you were certain that Matt had a crush on Mandy Anderson, and you were totally wrong. And before admitting your mistake, you had us running around looking for "clues" that he was in love with her!

Will: **Well . . . so?**

Cornelia: So, what is it this time? Little hearts fluttering above their heads, passionate hugs, and kisses of betrayal?

Will: **I am *not* overreacting! I saw Matt talking to some beautiful blonde.**

And he was smiling and laughing the whole time.

Cornelia: When did this big tragedy occur?

Will: Just a few minutes ago! I saw them on my way here. This time I'm not making things up – the two of them were totally making puppy-dog eyes at each other.

Taranee: Puppy-dog eyes? Is that all?

Will: Is that all? They were practically throwing themselves at each other – it was disgusting!

Cornelia: Will, I don't understand you. When it comes to Matt, you see things that simply are not there!

Will: Grrrrrr!

Hay Lin: My, my, aren't we sensitive.

Taranee: Hey, look who's coming our way!

Matt approaches the girls, flashing a big smile.

Cornelia (whispers to Will): Remember, stay calm!

Matt: Hi, everybody! Hi, Will!

Cornelia, Taranee, and Hay Lin: Hi, Matt!

Matt: Hey, Will, are you mad at me? You just rode past me on your bike and didn't even stop. I wanted to introduce you to my cousin Molly. She's visiting for a few days – I haven't seen her since last year! She would have loved to meet you. I've got to head right home, we're

having lunch with my aunt and uncle.
Bye! Bye, Will.

Cornelia, Taranee, and Hay Lin: **So long, Matt!**

After Matt leaves, the group throws Will the classic I-told-you-so glare.

Will: Don't say it! I know, I know. I was totally wrong. When the subject is Matt, I kinda overreact.

Cornelia: **No kidding! And you definitely don't hide it when you're annoyed. Couldn't you at least have said hi to Matt?**

Will: You're right, Corny! I guess I just can't help it! I like him so much, and I hate it when I think he might not like me.

Taranee: **I know what you mean, Will. When you really like somebody, it's normal to be jealous. While you wish you were always the center of attention, you view all the other girls as a possible threat. Try to remember, it won't be easy for him to find anyone better than you!**

Cornelia: And keep your cool. Sometimes you should keep your feelings of jealousy hidden. At least until you find out whether they're justified or not!

Will: **Are you guys finished?**

Cornelia and Taranee: Yes . . . Promise.

Hay Lin: **Can I add one thing?**

Will: Only if you're willing to speak in my favour! I don't think I can handle any more critiques.

Hay Lin: I just wanted to say that with a hunk like Matt, I'd be out-of-my-mind jealous, too!

THE ORACLE SAYS . . .

If you've got a short fuse when it comes to jealousy, it can be a mask for insecurity. Stop and think. Sometimes, the motivation behind certain behavior hides our needs to feel important, loved, and accepted – to be someone's "one and only."

DEAR WILL
Will has a huge heart and loves to give advice. Ask her your love questions, and you'll get some thoughtful answers!

Dear Will,
I think my best friend has a crush on my boyfriend. What should I do?
– Torn in Two

Dear Torn in Two,
Talk about a love triangle! I would try talking to your friend. Maybe she is just spending time with your boyfriend to be close to you.
Will

Dear Will,
I have a mega-crush on my friend's older brother. If I told my friend, she'd flip out. Help!
– Pining Away

Dear Pining Away,
Stop! Don't go there – your friend is bound to be your friend for the long haul. Don't risk making it uncomfortable for a fun, flirty, but brief crush.
Will

Dear Will,
I can't stand it when my crush talks to other girls.
How can I stop him from doing it?
– Jealous

Dear Jealous,
You can't! Sorry – but he is just your crush. Be patient and be your normal self, and when you become his girlfriend you'll know who he likes!  Will

WHAT CAN YOU DO IF . . .

You tend to get jealous when it comes to your crush?

• Try to maintain lots of your *own* interests. Keeping yourself occupied means you won't have time to be obsessed with where he is, whom he's with, and what he's doing!

• Don't call him three times a day unless you want it to look as if you're keeping tabs on him!

• Avoid interrogating him about what he's been up to. If you want to know, casually drop a question in the middle of your conversation like, "Did you end up going out yesterday afternoon?"

Your *boyfriend* is especially jealous?

• Don't give him any reason to be; avoid flirting with other guys.

• Don't lie to him. To a jealous guy, lying is the same as cheating – so be honest!

• Tell him that he's got to trust you and that he must control his feelings of jealousy; otherwise it could tear the two of you apart.

TEST
See How Romantic You Are

To find out what love means to you, begin with Question 1, and choose answer A or B. Then go to the question indicated by your answer. Get your profile, and read about your romance style.

1. Love is . . .
   A. Happiness.
      Go to Question 2.
   B. Tears.
      Go to Question 3.

2. The best way to catch a boy's eye is with . . .
   A. Looks.
      Go to Question 5.
   B. Personality.
      Go to Question 6.

3. When you like a boy, you are . . .
   A. Outgoing and flirty.
      Go to Question 4.
   B. Shy and quiet.
      Go to Question 6.

4. The boy of your dreams . . .
   A. Gives you lots of love and cuddles.
      Go to Profile B.
   B. Makes you feel superspecial.
      Go to Profile C.

5. Your biggest flaw is that . . .
   A. You're a daydreamer.
      Go to Profile A.
   B. You don't give yourself enough credit.
      Go to Profile D.

6. If the guy you like looks at you . . .
   A. You look back and give him a flirty smile.
      Go to Profile A.
   B. You pretend not to see him.
      Go to Profile D.

PROFILES
Profile A
Super romantic

Heart thumping loudly inside your chest, you're ready to fall in love at the drop of a hat, or to let yourself be won over just as quickly. You think love is supposed to be like in the movies, with moonlight rendezvous and sweet gifts.

ADVICE: It is wonderful to experience love as if it were a fairy tale with a happy ending. But just remember to keep your head on your shoulders – you can't confuse real life with the movies!

Profile B
Extra lovable

Love is something fun for you, a carefree adventure filled with laughter and tenderness, teddy bears, and private jokes. You want affection from the one you love, but you don't demand it.

ADVICE: Nice going! Keep up the healthy attitude toward love. Even if a broken heart comes sooner or later, with an outlook like yours, you'll get over it faster than the speed of light!

Profile C
Chronically insecure

You may think love is fantastic, but it also frightens you. You're afraid of letting your heart go, and you don't like depending on another person to make you happy.

ADVICE: Relax, let yourself go, and set your insecurities aside. Somewhere there's a super guy waiting for you, and when you meet him, you'll feel safe letting go.

Profile D
Super shy
Why does your heart shift into high gear every time you meet a guy you like? For you, love is a problem! Your shyness is an obstacle. The more you like a guy, the faster you want to hightail it every time you see him!
ADVICE: Take a deep breath the next time you see him coming, and don't worry about blushing – he'll probably find you all the more intriguing for it!

CHAPTER EIGHT
DEALING WITH A CHEATER

FROM HAY LIN'S DIARY

⚘ Monday

Big news: At my after-school French program (my parents thought it would be a good idea; i.e., they forced me to sign up!) I met Genny, a very sweet girl. We got into some great conversations. Sooner or later I'll have to introduce her to the girls! She's got a boyfriend, I think – only whenever she talks to him on her cell phone I've noticed she always winds up sad. I haven't asked her about it, because I don't want to seem overly curious . . . but I am curious!

⚘ Wednesday

This afternoon Genny called and asked me to go out with her. So we went for a walk together. She finally spilled the beans: now I understand why she's been so down – boy problems! She's afraid Evan, her boyfriend, is cheating on her! And frankly, judging from what she's told me, it sounds as if he is. Genny's crazy about him, and up until two weeks ago everything was going fine. Then there was this party they were supposed to go to together. But she was feeling a little sick, so he ended up going by himself. Since then Evan has been off in another world, grumpy and grouchy. Then Genny found out he's lied to her a couple times. Yesterday, for example, he told her he'd be hanging out during the evening with his band. But later, whom did Genny happen to meet by chance but his friends from the band? (Strange coincidence!) And Evan was nowhere to be found!

Today she asked him for an explanation, but he said he didn't want her checking up on him and that he didn't feel like talking about it. How awful! I don't know what to say to the girl. I don't think you should jump to conclusions in these cases, but it sounds as if Evan met another girl at the party. Genny's going to meet him tomorrow morning at school. Poor Genny! I wouldn't want to be in her shoes!

◎ *Monday*

The soap opera continues, with further tragic developments. Today Genny told me that she and Evan argued again yesterday. He claims there's no one else in his life and calls her paranoid. But after school one of Genny's friends told her that she saw Evan with another girl. Genny ran off in tears. I foresee serious trouble! I wish I could help her! But how?

◎ *Thursday*

Yesterday I spoke to the girls about Genny's problem. After a lengthy discussion, we all agreed on one thing: it's up to Genny to straighten out this situation. She shouldn't have to put up with that! And she shouldn't have to suffer!

◎ *Monday*

Today I spent the whole afternoon with Genny. I told her how I feel about her dilemma. Genny realises it's time to have it out with Evan once and for all! Even if it's not right to trust blindly in what other people go around saying, Evan owes her an explanation – at least for his strange behaviour and all the rumours going around about him.

⑥ *Sunday*

The soap opera has ended! They broke up! Here's what happened . . . Genny and Evan had a talk, and he admitted that something had changed between them. He also confessed that, yes, there was another girl involved, though it's "nothing important." After that he had the nerve to tell Genny he still liked her and didn't want to break up! At that point Genny told him to forget about it, that as far as she's concerned, they're through! Nice going, Genny – though she's one hurting puppy now. Which is understandable – she's still in love with the guy. If I were in her place, I'd want to count on my very best friends for support at a time like this. I think I'll introduce her to W.I.T.C.H. – we're sure to lend a hand in cheering the girl up. In fact, I think I'll get right on it! There's no time to waste when it comes to a great get-over-the-blues outing!

THE ORACLE SAYS ...

Never trust rumours – they may just be nasty lies made up by envious people. Don't lose faith in your boyfriend just because of gossip. If, however, you do happen to notice something strange in his behaviour, discuss it openly with him – it's a sign of maturity and self-respect on your part.

FIVE TIPS FOR HOW TO FIND OUT IF HE'S CHEATING ON YOU

WILL: I have my friends follow him!

IRMA: I ask him trick questions!

TARANEE: I trust my instincts!

CORNELIA: Is he telling lies? I check up on everything he says!

HAY LIN: I look him straight in the eye when I talk to him; if he's lying I'll catch him red-handed!

DEAR TARANEE

Taranee is quiet, but she has lots of good advice. With her help, boyfriend issues seem like a piece of cake!

Dear Taranee,
My parents don't trust my boyfriend. What should I do?
– Family Feud

Dear Family Feud,
It's natural for your parents to be cautious about boyfriends – after all, you're their little girl! Give them time, and they will come around. Just make sure he's worth the wait.
✳ Taranee

Dear Taranee,
My parents are sick of hearing me talk about my boyfriend. Any suggestions?
– Chatty in Love

Dear Chatty in Love,
Start talking about somebody else's boyfriend. Seriously though, do ease up. You don't want your parents to have any reason to be annoyed by your boyfriend.
✳ Taranee

Dear Taranee,
How can I convince my dad to trust my boyfriend?
– Help!

Dear Help!,
Try doing something with the two of them; maybe they'll bond. And if you're there they will already have something in common.
✳ Taranee

Dear Taranee,
My folks are always giving my boyfriend the third
degree. How can I make them stop?
– On Trial

Dear On Trial,
I think in this case, honesty is the best policy. Let them know it makes you *and* your boyfriend uncomfortable. Maybe they'll ease up.
✳ Taranee

CHAPTER NINE

BOYS TALK ABOUT GIRLS

⑤ *Tuesday*
At the Cooks' house

Peter, Nigel, Matt, and Eric are writing an article for the sports section of the school paper. Martin comes along wearing an annoyed expression.

Peter: What's up, Martin? You look beat.

Martin: I am! Let me tell you, the worst thing you can ever do is argue with a girl!

Nigel: No kidding. It's impossible to win!

Peter: Yo, Martin – are you referring to Irma Lair, by any chance?

Martin: You guessed it.

Peter: Don't let it get to you, dude!

Martin: I just can't seem to please her. Whatever I say is wrong.

Eric: What do you mean? What happened?

Martin: All I did was ask her to the Happy Bears meeting. I figured it was something she'd get a kick out of. They're really great. . . .

Eric: Sure . . .

Nigel: Well, what did she say?

Matt: "In your dreams, Martin!"

Eric: Ouch! Girls are so hard to figure out. Who knows what's going on in their minds?

Peter: Really, you can never tell how they're going to react! And I've got proof. Hold on a sec!

Peter goes into Taranee's room and comes back with a box.

Peter: Here are some pictures Taranee took of her friends. They are hilarious!

Martin: Peter, what if your sister comes home?

Peter: Take it easy, Martin! She won't be back before dinner. My friends, you are about to view absolute, photographic proof that girls are incomprehensible creatures. . . . Look! *(He holds up a picture.)* I call this

Miss Cornelia "I'm-Not-Having-Any-Fun-At-All!" Hale.

Peter: I had three tickets for the basketball finals, and I invited Taranee and Cornelia to go with me. Some people would have paid in gold for those seats. And yet Cornelia spent practically the whole match pouting! All she could say was, "How much longer?" and, "All this racket is getting on my nerves!" How could she not have had fun at that game?

Nigel: **Unbelievable!**

Matt: Hey, Peter, get a load of this! *(He holds up a picture of the girls watching a movie.)*

Nigel: **A chick-flick marathon! Who knows why, but all you have to do is plop two girls down in front of a screen showing two sappy lovebirds, and they fall to pieces!**

Peter: It's crazy! Their biggest thrill is a stupid romance, while they couldn't care less about being in the stands for a basketball championship! I swear, I'll never figure girls out. . . .

Eric: Look at this! A picture of Will . . .

Matt: That's the outfit Will wore to the dance! When I told her how great she looked, she replied that she'd just thrown on the first thing she could find.

Eric: Classic reply! You didn't fall for it, I hope?

Peter: When it comes to parties, girls can spend an entire day trying to find the right thing to wear. Then comes the try-on sessions with their friends. I'm up on all that stuff, because every time my sister and her friends have a party to go to, I hear the entire thing. And if there's one thing I'll

never do, it's go shopping with a girl!

Matt: It's funny how different boys and girls really are!

Nigel: You said it!

Matt: Well, we need to play it cool and keep our distance. When it comes to love, you've got to be tough!

Eric: Look who's talking. . . . Whenever Will asks you to do something, you act like a puppy dog.

Matt: The thing about Will is, even if she sometimes acts weird and drives me crazy, she's really cool and sweet. All she has to do is look at me with those eyes of hers. . . .

Nigel: And you can't resist!

Matt: You can't say no!

Eric: She's got you in the palm of her hand! Let's admit it once and for all: there's no sense in playing the tough guy, because even though girls are like creatures from another planet, creatures that we cannot understand in the slightest . . .

Matt, Nigel, Peter, and Martin: But that are impossible to live without!

THE ORACLE SAYS . . .

Even if boys and girls don't always see eye to eye, it is important to remember that we are all capable of the same feelings. Every time you and your girlfriends sit around thinking guys just don't get you, remember, you may not entirely get them either! Be patient, and with a little time (and a lot of talking), you will someday learn the language of boys – I hope!

CHAPTER TEN
LOVEBIRDS ON DISPLAY

⑥ *Saturday afternoon*
Heatherfield Park

Hay Lin: Girls, I've got an idea! What do you say
to an exhibition of hilarious "lovey-
dovey" faces?

Cornelia: Let's see if I got this straight. You want to
choose and put on display the faces we
make when we're with boys? You're crazy!

Hay Lin: Only the faces we make with *certain*
boys! Don't worry, it'll be an *extremely
private* exhibition!

Taranee: The mere thought of it makes me want to
annihilate you, but . . . come to think of it,

I like the idea! I can't wait to see Nigel's
face!

Irma: **This is going to be awesome! Hay Lin, I
can't wait to see Cornelia's face when
she's with Peter! What a hoot!**

Hay Lin: Okay, girls, everything will be ready in four
days!

Couldn't care less
i.e., May I be swallowed by a whale before I go out with him!

Too shy
i.e., Glances too hot to handle!

Green-eyed monster
i.e., Grrr . . . one more step and I'll destroy her!

Shocking
i.e., Why me?!

Hay Lin: Well, girls, what do you think?

Irma: I wouldn't show those pictures to anybody!

Cornelia: Well done, but personally, I deny everything! Which reminds me, we've got something for you too, Hay Lin. Whip it out, Taranee. . . .

And this is our contribution! Ha-ha!

Will: Not a bad shot. Right, Hay Lin?

Hay Lin: **Hand over the negative, now!**

Irma: Remember, the photo is mightier than the . . . sword!

Will, Taranee, and Cornelia: **Well said, Irma!**

TEST
Is He the Right Boy for You?

Answer the questions to find out whether the boy of your dreams is a Prince Charming or . . . a frog!

1. What was the first thing about him that caught your attention?
    - A. His behaviour
    - B. His expression
    - C. His smile
    - D. His body

2. When you're with him . . .
    - A. You forget everything else!
    - B. You're happy.
    - C. You're fine . . . though sometimes a little bored!
    - D. You feel embarrassed.

3. You have similar tastes, especially when it comes to . . .
    - A. Ideas – you view the world in the same way!
    - B. Music and movies.
    - C. Clothes.
    - D. Nothing! You're total opposites!

4. You like him because . . .
   A. He knows how to listen to you.
   B. He makes you laugh!
   C. He's different from the other boys.
   D. He's supercute!

5. When you're feeling down . . .
   A. He always knows how to cheer you up.
   B. He tries to distract you.
   C. He has no idea how to handle it.
   D. He doesn't even realise it.

6. When you're together with friends . . .
   A. He's relaxed and makes sure you are, too.
   B. He's always himself!
   C. He doesn't pay attention
      to you.
   D. He puts you down and
      then pretends it's funny.

ANSWERS

You chose mostly *A* answers.

Prince Charming

Can there be any further doubt? You were made for each other. You've got the starring roles in a beautiful love story. There's a perfect understanding between the two of you. You share secrets, enjoy being together, and can talk to each other nonstop for hours!

You chose mostly *B* answers.

Wait and See!

He's a total cutie, but you're still not 100 percent sure. Sometimes you like him a lot, other times he gets on your nerves! Don't worry, this happens sometimes. You just need to take the time to become more clear about your feelings. After all, maybe he's really just a good friend. On the other hand, he could be the man of your dreams. Wait and see!

You chose mostly C answers.

Where Are the Sparks?

You two share magical moments of togetherness, but only when things are supersmooth between you. As for the rest of the time, forget it. He may be cute, but he doesn't understand you and doesn't know how to relate to you. Besides those lovely big eyes of his, there's not much else about him that turns you to mush. Keep searching and dreaming, and sooner or later you, too, will find your Prince Charming!

You chose mostly D answers.

A Real Frog!

You may love amphibians, poor girl, but this guy is slimier than what you had in mind! And too bad that old kissing trick won't transform this frog into a handsome prince! He tends to treat you like a second-class citizen, especially in front of his friends. Don't sweat it. There are loads of kind, cute guys out there just dying to meet you! Repeat the following chant to yourself at least ten times daily: *"Down with frogs! Up with princes!"*

THE TOP TEN GOLDEN RULES FOR DEALING WITH BOYFRIENDS

1. Don't bend over backward for him, even if you're head over heels in love.

2. Always try to be sincere, even if sometimes the truth hurts.

3. Try not to appear different from what you really are just to please him.

4. Don't cling.

5. Don't neglect your friends on account of him.

6. Remember that cute, smart, kind boys are better than boys who are just cute.

7. Treat him the way you want to be treated.

8. Voice any objections you may have. . . . Honesty is the best policy.

9. Never put him on a pedestal. . . . Those are for statues!

10. Trust him, but also trust yourself!

HE LOVES ME, HE LOVES ME NOT?

Do you often find yourself wondering whether he really loves you? Check below to see!

He likes you.

- He constantly tries to make eye contact with you.

- He smiles at you, even when a smile may seem inappropriate!

- He plays with his hair in your presence.

- He fiddles nervously with any object that happens to be within reach when you are near.

He doesn't like you.

- His body language reveals a closed attitude toward you – arms folded or leaning away from you.

- He avoids all physical contact with you.

- He doesn't go out of his way to find things the two of you have in common.

- He avoids making eye contact with you.

WHAT CAN YOU DO IF . . .

You find it hard to act natural and be yourself when you're with a boy?

● Remember that, generally speaking, boys are actually frightened out of their wits by girls, though they may not show it. No matter how bold they may seem, don't let boys overpower you.

● Don't become obsessed – you'll see that in time you, too, will learn to relax around boys.

You think you're not cute enough for boys to like you (even though that is just not true)?

● Don't focus on what you perceive as physical defects. Boys aren't that fussy, and besides, a pimple here or there never frightened off any boy!

● Keep in mind that physical beauty isn't everything, and that possessing a bright and lively personality will attract more boys than even a basketball game or a skateboarding contest could.

You're really into him, but your friends can't stand the guy?

- Talk to each of your friends about it one-on-one, and explain how happy you are with him. That way, if they really care about you, they'll be happy for you and respect your choice!

- Try to get him to spend more time with your friends; they're sure to see him in a whole new light!

SAY, "I LOVE YOU" ALL AROUND THE WORLD!

Albanian	*Te dua*
Croatian	*Volim te*
Czech	*Miluji te*
Danish	*Jeg Elsker Dig*
Dutch	*Ik hou van jou*
Finnish	*Minä rakastan sinua*
French	*Je t'aime*
German	*Ich liebe dich*
Greek	*S'agapo*
Hungarian	*Szeretlek*
Italian	*Ti amo*
Norwegian	*Jeg Elsker Deg*
Polish	*Kocham Cie*

Portuguese	*Eu te amo*
Romanian	*Te iubesc*
Russian	*Ya tebya liubliu*
Slovak	*Lubim ta*
Spanish	*Te amo*
Swedish	*Jag älskar dig*
Turkish	*Seni seviyorum*